CHAKRA CLEARING COLORING BOOK WITH THE ARCHANGELS

A GUIDED MEDITATION WITH THE ANGELS IN ACTION

LUCIA COCHRAN

BALBOA.PRESS

A DIVISION OF HAY HOUSE

Balboa Press books may be ordered through booksellers or by contacting:

Balboa Press
A Division of Hay House
1663 Liberty Drive
Bloomington, IN 47403
www.balboapress.com
844-682-1282

Print information available on the last page.

Interior Graphics/Art Credit: Illustrations by David Cochran

ISBN: 979-8-7652-4418-0 (sc)
ISBN: 979-8-7652-4417-3 (e)

Balboa Press rev. date: 08/15/2023

CONTENTS

INTRODUCTION

Hello

My name is Lucia Cochran

I am an Angel communicator, psychic, medium, Heart Math Resilience Advantage Facilitator, I offer past life clearings, SRT, (Spiritual Response Practitioner), and hair salon owner.

I have a private practice now for over 20 years.

I offer sessions on Mondays in person when my hair salon is closed and via Zoom on Thursdays.

All my sessions are guided by the Angelic realm, no matter what I am offering during a session.

Angel = 'Messenger of God'

We 'pray to God', our Divine Creator of all that is and ever was.

The 'Force that flows through everyone and everything.

We 'call upon the Angels'.

The Angels assist, guide, protect, heal and support us during this physical existence, that is if we choose to call upon them.

They will not interfere with our free will. We must call upon them and invite them into our lives to have them assist us.

If there happens to be a life-threatening situation they may intercede.

Over the years I have been guided by the angels to offer Chakra Clearings during my sessions with their assistance.

Chakras

Chakras are the energy centers of our bodies.

They are in the astral body, along our spines.

They start at the base of the spine and continue upwards to the top/crown of the head.

Our astral body is the energy body that is inside our physical body.

Each physical body part has a corresponding astral body part.

We cannot see the energy, but it exists.

Our Chakras are energetic wheels/discs.

There are 7 major Chakras.

The chakras have a specific color and energy that they radiate.

Each one coincides with a gland in the physical body as well.

Each chakra relates to specific spiritual, emotional, psychological, and physical aspects of our being.

It is believed that when there is a blockage or malfunction in one of these energy centers, it can lead to physical, psychological, and emotional disorders.

When a chakra is blocked, not spinning properly and/or cloudy or not shining brightly, that area in you life that it represents may be blocked and not working properly as well.

It is said that when we balance these energy centers, on the other hand, is believed to lead to well-being and good health and balance in the areas of our lives that they represent.

There is a wealth of information on the Angels and the chakras on the internet and other avenues.

I have developed my own system in my sessions and clearing by working with the angels through their guidance.

Together we developed a very special and unique relationship over the years.

They have made their presence apparent to me in my personal life in my darkest hours and have pulled me into the light on numerous occasions.

Presented me with opportunities and the insight to recognize them as they come.

This coloring book has been guided to me during a session with a client. The message was for me.

I have been blessed to have my Son David Cochran, the artist and creator of all the illustrations in this book, by my Side the entire way.

My husband Dan Cochran has been my support system in all my crazy ventures over the years and I could not be more grateful. He is my best friend and love of my life.

This coloring book is the chakra clearing meditation that I have developed.

As you color each chapter of this book, you will be clearing the chakra that the chapter is about.

I highly recommend listening to meditation while coloring, or at least do it once a day first thing in the morning before you start your day.

There is an explanation on why David chose each image and the meaning behind it.

I am so excited and blessed to be sharing this gift with you all.

I hope you enjoy it!

The Angels and Archangels have been a significant part of my life for over 25 years.

During this time, I have been working closely with them on all my endeavors and in all areas of my life.

They assist, guide, protect, heal, and encourage us whenever we call upon them to do so.

The Archangels that I have presented in this coloring book channeled their loving guidance and healing through me years ago. They often teach me different ways to work with them.

I have been blessed with the ability to hear, feel, see, think, and know what they are presenting to me.

It is essential to connect to the 'Source' that **is all.**

The best time to do this is first thing when you wake up in the morning, and at bedtime.

This will anchor you as you go about your day.

You will find that you are able to observe outside distractions and discordance instead of being dragged into lower vibrational activities.

This makes you more of a clear channel of information from the 'Divine' and makes your ability to 'connect' to the Angels and their guidance much stronger.

They are the 'Messengers of our Creator and exist to help us on our Earthly journey and they are waiting for us to call on them.

All the Archangels have a frequency and vibration and color associated with them.

They all have a 'task' or area in life that they are responsible for and that they work on for us when called upon.

You will see, in this coloring book the Archangels that I have presented and how they have guided me to work with them when clearing the chakra system.

I have called upon more than one to clear some of the chakras and only one of them in other chakras.

I have been guided to call upon Michael and Gabriel more than once in the meditation.

Here is a definition of them below and how they work with me while clearing each chakra.

Enjoy!

Scan the QR code to hear the meditation. It is recommended to listen to it while coloring the images in this book for a thorough chakra clearing. Enjoy!

CHAKRA CLEARING MEDITATION

Sit comfortably in a chair as you, place your awareness and attention into the area of your heart.

Imagine that your breath is flowing in and out of the center of your heart.

Breathing a little slower and deeper than unusual, feeling your breath flowing in and out of the area of your heart.

Allow your breath to be a little slower and deeper than normal as you are breathing in and out of your heart.

Now, attempt to activate and sustain an elevated emotion, such as joy, happiness, or gratitude for someone or something that you love and care for in your life.

Allow that feeling to radiate in your heart.

Imagine and allow that feeling to radiate throughout your entire body.

Love, gratitude, joy, radiating, expanding throughout your entire body.

Feel it in every cell of your being & throughout your entire body.

Take a moment now to imagine that feeling expanding beyond your body and reaching out into the room that you are sitting in.

As you feel your breath and this elevated emotion flowing through your body, you notice you feel lighter and at peace.

Imagine now a beautiful white light flickering in the center of your being.

This is like the light of a furnace pilot light.

This is the light of your soul.

On every inhalation and on every exhalation this light is expanding and filling up your entire being.

Filling your torso, your trunk, seat, thighs, knees, shins and calves.

It's filling up your feet and toes.

Allow it to flow as it starts working its way back up into your trunk, as this light is filling up your chest and your neck and your shoulders.

It now works way down your arms, your hands and fingers.

It is engulfing and surrounding you as you feel it working its way up into your neck and your head.

Imagine this white light in the space behind your eyes, behind your nose, your eyes, lips, mouth and between your ears.

You are feeling lighter and more at peace.

You are now connected to the eternal being that you truly are.

Now,

Put your awareness on the base of your spine your root chakra energy center.

Imagine a beautiful ruby, red earth energy fan of light, spinning, shining, and glowing at the base of your spine in the root chakra energy center, as you call upon Archangel Michael, Archangel, Nathaniel and Archangel Ariel.

We call upon you heavenly beings to clear balance, harmonize, and bless the root chakra energy center as you wash away and remove any fears, worries, concerns, and blocks, regarding money, income, nurturing, survival needs, life path and life purpose, security and resources.

Clear balance, harmonize and bless the root chakra energy center.

Archangel Michael, Nathaniel, and Ariel.

Thank you.

Place your awareness below your navel as you move your awareness to the sacral chakra energy center.

Imagine and visualize a beautiful, orange fan of light, spinning, shining, and glowing in the sacral chakra as you call upon Archangel Gabriel.

Archangel Gabriel, please clear away any fears, worries or concerns in my life related to creativity, balance, intimacy, and desires.

Clear any blocks to producing in my life and allow me to create what it is that I desire and experience.

Infuse me with balance and creativity.

Thank you, Gabriel, for clearing, balancing harmonizing, and blessing my sacral chakra energy center.

Place your awareness in your solar plexus in the center of your being.

Actively visualize a beautiful yellow, sun like golden fan of light, spinning, shining, and glowing in your center as you call upon Archangel Uriel.

Archangel Uriel, please remove any fears, worries or concerns regarding personal power, confidence, courage, self-esteem, and transformation in my life.

Infuse me with divine intelligence as you clear away fears, worries or concerns in any of these areas in my life as you infuse me with the courage to accept these gifts.

Allow me to experience transformation, Divine intelligence, personal power, confidence, and courage as I navigate through each day on my earthly journey.

Thank you Archangel Uriel.

Place your awareness to the area of your heart.

Now, imagine a beautiful emerald, green fan of light spinning, shining and glowing as you call upon Archangel Raphael.

Archangel Raphael, please remove any fears, blocks, worries, or concerns regarding love.

Allow me to love myself enough to be loved and attract the love that I desire.

Please heal all wounds and areas in my life regarding Love.

Infuse me with healing white light love and protection, healing my body heart, soul, and mind.

Archangel Raphael allow me to give love and receive love freely as I learn to trust, but not blindly,

Healing all areas in my life regarding **love**.

Thank you, Archangel Raphael.

Place your awareness in your throat chakra energy center.

Around the area of your throat.

Now, imagine a beautiful sky-blue fan of light, spinning, shining, and glowing as you call upon Archangel Haniel, and once again, Gabriel.

Haniel & Gabriel, please remove any fears, blocks, worries, or concerns regarding communication.

Allow me to speak my truth, and to be heard.

Please clear away any miscommunication regarding delivering my words and expressing myself in a peaceful and harmonious and effective manner.

Archangel Haniel to help me to express myself through the Grace of our Creator.

Archangel Gabriel, messenger of God, allow my words to be understood with clarity and purpose!

Clear, balance, harmonize and bless my throat chakra energy center.

Thank you Archangel Haniel and Gabriel.

Place your awareness to the space between your eyebrows, the brow chakra energy center.

Imagine a beautiful cobalt blue fan of light, spinning, shining, and glowing in the center of your brow.

Once again call upon Archangel Michael.

Archangel Michael with your legions of angels and fiery sword of light, please remove any fears worries or concerns regarding seeing.

Allow me to see clearly, visualize, and have the insight and clarity of the path that is presented before me.

Give me vision and insight and clarity in all areas of my life as you remove any blocks and concerns regarding vision, intuition, and psychic abilities.

Clear, harmonize and bless the brow chakra energy center.

Thank you Archangel Michael.

Place your awareness to the top of your head, the crown chakra energy center.

Imagine a beautiful violet fan of light spinning, shining and glowing as we call upon archangel Metatron with his Merkabah cube.

Archangel Metatron, please clear, balance, harmonize, and bless my crown chakra energy center as you remove any fears worries or concerns regarding healing, seeing thinking, hearing and knowing information that is being divinely guided to me from the light of the Lord and my divine team.

Metatron, allow me to feel, see, think, hear, and know the information, that is being divinely guided to me from the light of the Lord.

Give me the knowledge, wisdom and understanding to download, process and assimilate it all.

Balance, harmonize, and bless me.

Connect me to the heavens and ground me to the Earth.

Balance and harmonize all of my chakras.

Thank you, Archangel Metatron.

Thank you, God for sending me you beautiful angels, archangels, guardian angels, my Divine Team, and the Holy Spirit to clear, balance and harmonize my life.

Thank you for my connection to the divine that lives within me, for I am eternal.

Thank you for the assistance and gifts in my life with this beautiful connection to your heavenly love.

Stay connected to this place of love and light within you, as you are on this journey in your garments of flesh.

Blessings to all.

Lucia Cochran

Root Chakra-Saturn

Saturn is known to be the planet of structure, authority, responsibility, boundaries, and limits. It is also associated with the physical realm such as our material possessions, survival instinct, resources, and security.

Sacral Chakra-Jupiter

Jupiter is the planet of spirituality, of philosophy, of expansion, faith, & optimism. The openness of Jupiter is related to open creativity and life balance. This also relates to your appetites and desires.

Solar Plexus Chakra-Mars & Sun

Mars represents confidence, self-discipline, ambition, and leadership. The Solar Plexus Chakra helps us to act and follow through on our goals. Mars gives us determination and courage to take on difficult tasks.

The Sun has energy that helps to motivate us and gives us a sense of purpose.

They both help us develop our leadership skills and make sure we take action to reach our goals.

They also give us the strength to assert ourselves.

Heart Chakra-Venus

The planet Venus represents feminine energy, love, passion, pleasure, and beauty.

Venus helps us in all relationships, including self-love. Connecting to Venus we can open to new possibilities that allow us to heal and grow. Align with this planet for a deeper understanding of love, connection, joy, and balance in your life.

Throat Chakra-Mercury

Mercury is known to be the planet of self-expression, authentic communication and purity of speech as well. It also is responsible for mental clarity.

Brow Chakra-Moon

The moon is considered to be the earth's natural satellite.

It shines by the sun's reflected light as it brings light to darkness on earth so that we may see at night.

Crown Chakra-Universe/Solar System

Representing, the All-encompassing and connection to the 'Divine.'

Connects to the heavens and grounds to the earth.

Root Chakra

Michael: "Who is like God."

Michael battles evil, challenges people who have evil or negative intentions, and helps people open to new ways of thinking, bringing courage for spiritual experiences. He is our protector and washes away fears and blocks that keep us from living a joyous, abundant, fulfilling life when called upon.

Nathaniel: "Gift of God."

His presence in our lives is mainly to transform us, give us life purpose and helps us manifest. He rules over the sun and the stars. He has an extremely powerful energy that is rapid and passionate, working to motivate us, protect us, and purify us. When he releases his energy, it hits the deepest point in our hearts. This brings out passion and courage. He helps us to leave our zones of comfort and work hard to attain purpose in our lives

Ariel: "Lion or lioness of God."

She is Known as the archangel of the earth and works tirelessly on behalf of the planet. She oversees the elemental kingdom and helps in the healing of animals, especially the non-domesticated kind. She is strongly connected to earth energy and connecting to the 'Divine' that flows through our beautiful planet.

Sacral Chakra

Gabriele: "Man/Messenger of God."

Gabriel announces God's plans and actions. He brought forth the news of Jesus. He will tell you about your path and purpose and will send help to 'create' in your life. He will assist with balance, appetites, and desires as well as assist in attracting, "Beauty, love, happiness, pleasure, and harmony in your life when called upon.

Solar Plexus Chakra

Uriel: "God is light."

Uriel will light upon a troubling situation, which illuminates your problem-solving abilities. Call upon Uriel whenever you get into a sticky situation, and you need to think clearly and find answers. Uriel also helps students and those who need intellectual assistance. He infuses us with confidence, courage and personal power.

Heart Chakra

Raphael: "God has overcome/He who heals."

He works with healers and artists and is helpful to creative souls. Messages from Raphael may help you to focus on creating a space of beauty, a recognition of the beauty that surrounds you, and the healing energy that comes from embracing such beauty. All areas in life and of love are healed when we call upon Raphael.

Throat Chakra

Haniel: "Grace of God."

Call upon her whenever you wish to add grace and its effects (peace, serenity, enjoyment of good friends' company, beauty, harmony, and so on) to your life. She will also assist you before any event in which you desire to be the embodiment of grace, such as giving an important presentation, being interviewed for a job, or going on a first date when called upon.

Crown Chakra

Metatron: "One who guards."

Metatron was the Hebrew prophet, Enoch. One of the only angels that walked earth and lived a perfect life of conduct to ascend.

He became an ascended master and God transformed him into the powerful Archangel. He is one of the most powerful archangels in this New Age because he directly represents our capacity for ascension and our ability to access spiritual power. You may ask for Metatron's help to discover their personal spiritual power and learn how to use it to bring glory to God and make the world a better place. Call upon him to directly represent your capacity for ascension and ability to access your spiritual power. In the field of sacred geometry, it is known that Metatron oversees the flow of energy in a mystical light cube known as a Merkabah or Metatron's Cube. His cube contains the geometric shapes in God's creation and represents the patterns that makeup everything God has made for us.

CHAPTER 1

ROOT CHAKRA

- Primal Energy
  - olcano: Much like the root chakra is the primal energy center, the volcano could be considered to be one of the most primal energy sources from the earth. The molten lava within it is drawn directly from the mantle, below the earth's crust, and flows up and out to the surface.

- Earth
  - Landscape: One of the main purposes of the root chakra is to link us to the earth. When we are patient and resourceful with the many aspects of our lives this chakra anchors us to the earth, grounding us and keeping a strong spiritual connection to the natural world.

CHAPTER 2

SACRAL CHAKRA

- Sexuality –
  - In ancient Latin cultures, the process of human sex represented in art was derived from agricultural and horticultural life. Fruit such as apples represented the male genitalia.
  - In Sigmund Freud's psychoanalytical research, he found that in interpreting imagery in dreams, things like little cases, and boxes represent the female counterpart

- Creativity
  - Light bulb – The light bulb is a popular symbol of creativity, also meant to represent a new idea or sudden inspiration. This is the same with the use of the bolt of lightning
  - The Brain – Carrying out creative functions and new way of thinking and acting are fundamental functions of the brain
  - Awen – An important Celtic symbol representing creativity, imagination, and aesthetic sensibility. The word "Awen" means essence or inspiration in the Celtic language and it is believed that the Awen would turn into a muse and instigate creativity among artists

- Balance
  - The ancient Egyptians believed that your heart held in it the entirety of the deeds throughout your life, good and bad. When you died, your heart would be weighed against the feather of Maat, the goddess of truth and justice. If the heart was in balance with the weight of the feather, you would be allowed entrance into the afterlife.

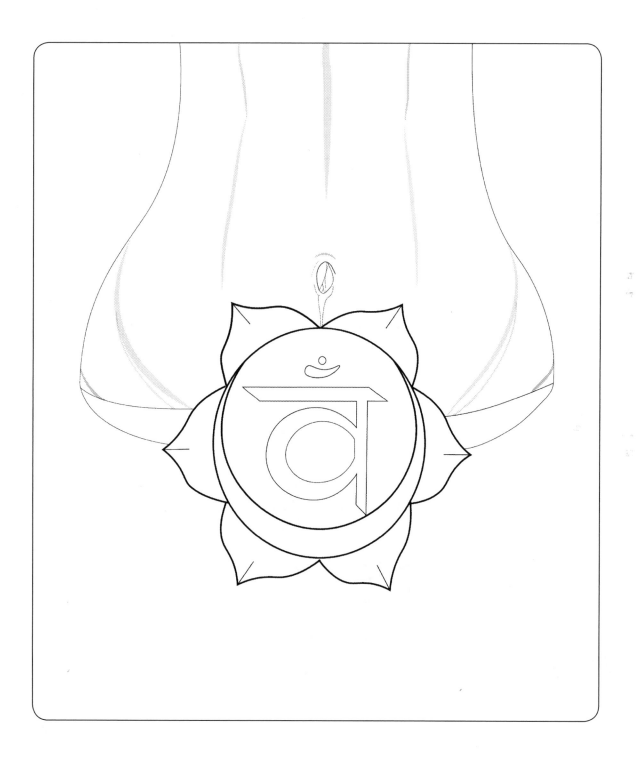

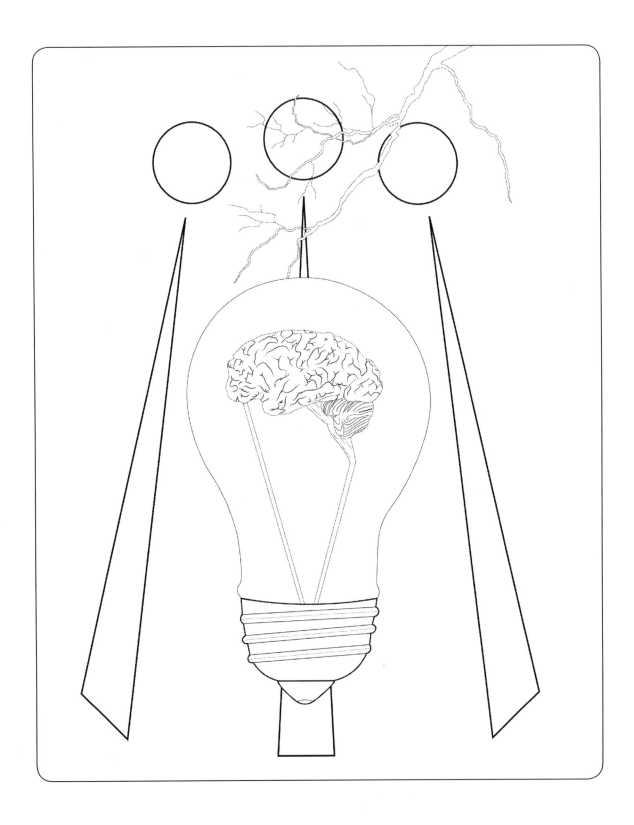

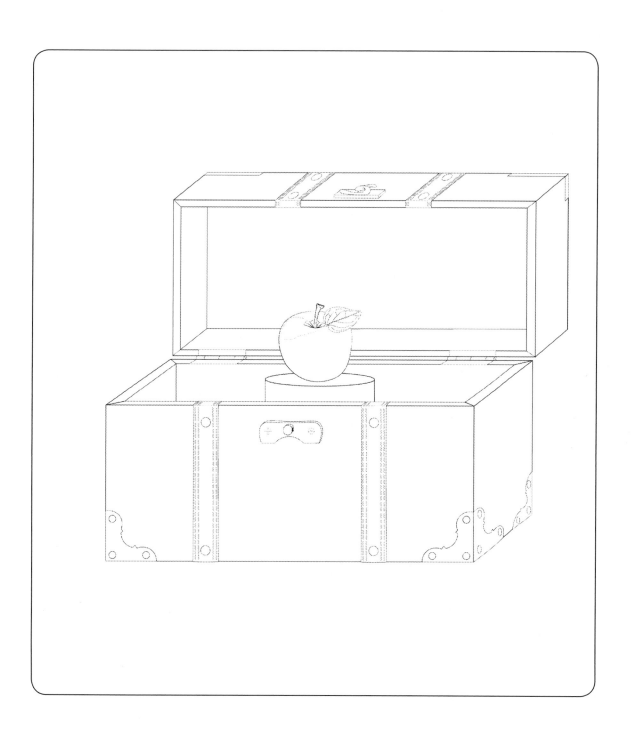

CHAPTER 3

SOLAR PLEXUS CHAKRA

- Transformation
  - Iris Flower - Since they are planted before or during winter and bloom in the spring, the Iris are known to represent change and recovery.
  - Dragonfly – The dragonfly is meant to personify the versatility of change experienced through everyday life. The specific element of the dragonfly attributes to overwhelming change that is able to take place one step at a time.

- Strong Ego/Self Awareness
  - When describing the Ego in relation to the Id, Sigmund Freud described it as similar to a man on the back of horse. The man in this case would be the Ego, and the horse the Id. Like it is the job of the man to control the greater strength of the horse and guide it in the proper direction, it is the job of the Ego with its ability to rationalize to control the more powerful primal instincts and desires of the Id to achieve a realistic plan of action.

- Courage
  - Lion – being at the top of their food chain in the savanna, lions are a fearless predator and in turn are often used to represent the virtues of courage and bravery.
  - Uruz – The rune uruz is an ancient Nordic symbol. Known as the rune of the inner-king and inner-queen, this rune is said to govern one's assertion of their independence as well as their courage, strength, and persistence against all odds.

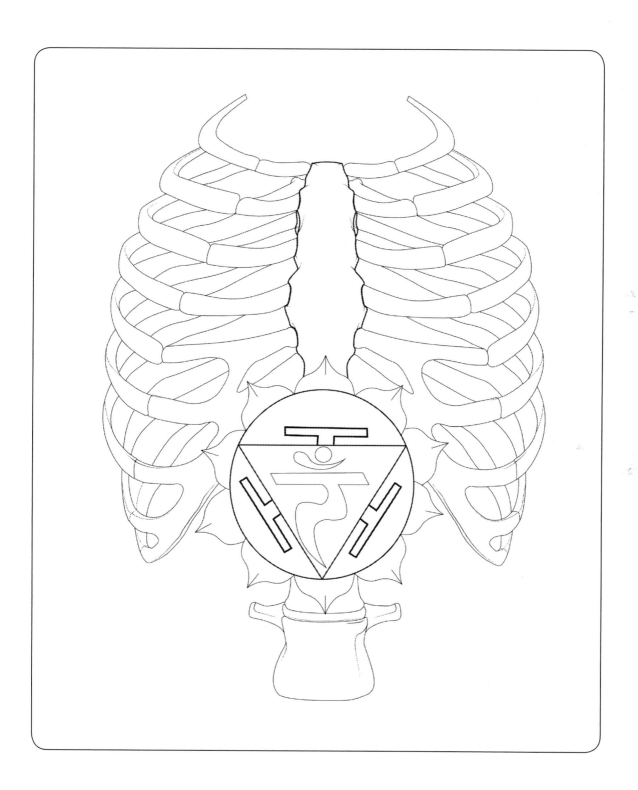

CHAPTER 4

HEART CHAKRA

- Love
  - Harp: Within Celtic culture, the harp was thought to be the bridge of love that connected the heaven and earth and in Norway and Iceland, they likened the harp's strings to the rungs of a ladder that one could use to ascend into the higher aspects of love.
  - Dove: Being that they mate with one another for life, doves have long been considered representative of love. The history of the dove's use dates as far back to ancient Greece, where Greek mythology often depicted the goddess of love, Aphrodite, with doves in flight around her if not resting upon her person.
  - Shell: The hard outer casing of the seashell conceals and safeguards the prized pearl within. As a result, the shell has developed into as a symbol to represent love of the protective nature.

- Peace
  - Olive Branch: The olive branch is used as a sign of peace throughout western civilization. The origin of its use is believed to date back to the ancient Greek's, who along with believing that the olive tree was a representation of abundance, used the olive branch to serve as a key attribute to Eirene, the goddess of peace.
  - Paper Crane: In Japanese culture, the crane has long been considered to be a symbol of luck. According to Japanese folk lore, it is said that anyone who manages to fold a thousand origami cranes will have one of their wishes fulfilled. With that tale in mind, a Japanese girl named Sadako Sasaki, who had developed radiation-induced leukemia as a result of the bombing of Hiroshima, set out to achieve that. All in with the hopes that she would be cured of her disease. When she died in 1955 at the age of 12, Sasaki had managed to fold 644 cranes. The task was then completed by her friends and family, and the thousand paper cranes were then buried with her. Ever since, the symbol of the paper crane been considered a symbol of peace and for anti-war and anti-nuclear movements.
  - Deer/Doe: Within Buddhism, the deer is known to symbolize harmony, happiness, peace and longevity. Since they are by nature a timid and gentle animal, their presence in a place represents the clarity of region free of fear.

- Trust
  - Wax Seal: Once the wax seal is dried, it was impossible for the letter it enclosed to be opened without breaking it. Therefore, if the seal was broken upon arrival, it meant that an individual that was not meant to see the letter had done so, and there a had been a breach of trust.
  - Elephants: Elephants are known to possess a good memory. They remember other elephants and even humans that they have encountered. This strong sense of memory allows them to remain faithful to their companions for a long time. Because of this, they are strongly associated to trustworthiness.
  - Claddagh: The claddagh ring is a traditional Irish ring that symbolizes feelings of trust, love, and friendship. It features two hands holding a heart at the center, adorned with a crown on top. The pair of hands represent friendship, the heart is a symbol of love, and the crown on top is associated with complete loyalty and dedication.

CHAPTER 5

THROAT CHAKRA

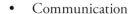

- Communication
  - Bee: Bees represent communication as well as organization, abundance, and productivity. Bees are extremely intelligent creatures who have evolved to use 3 complex methods in which they communicate with one another. One of the simplest methods they utilize is through touch. By making contact with the antennae of another, bees are able to identify one another. Another mode of communication is in their use of pheromones, which queen, drone and worker bees all are using all the time to maintain a state a constant state of communication with the entire hive. Not only these, but bees also dance as a means to communicate with one another. They do a figure eight type dance, called the waggle, in order to convey the location of pollen and nectar. The rest of the hive will then vote on how viable a discovered location is by joining in with the dance with a specific intensity.
  - Fountain Pen: Not only does the fountain pen represent the ability to communicate through the utilization of the written word, but the use of ink represents the specified intent and permanence of the words one chooses to put to the page.
- Truth
  - Mirror: A mirror shows the viewer exactly the way something exists. It can never lie; it simply reflects the reality of what lies before it. Because of this mirrors have been frequently used in literature as means to symbolize truth.
  - Dharma Wheel: The word 'Dharma', means truth in Sanskrit, and the dharma wheel is known to represent the teachings of the Buddha and his guidelines on the path to enlightenment.

- Integrity
  - Moose: The moose is one of the largest members of the deer family, and they are known to possess a watchful and stable disposition which attributes them to their representation of integrity. In some Native American cultures, young boys were instructed to attain a moose totem for their transition into adulthood. It was thought that the moose would grant them physical fortitude as well as mental clarity and good character.
  - Bamboo: Bamboo is one of the tallest growing species of grass in the world and is well known for its flexibility and shocking durability. It is capable of growing and flourishing despite rugged terrain. Like the way a man of good character is both strong in his beliefs yet able to alter his perspective when presented with new information, bamboo is both strong and flexible making it a strong symbol of the virtue of integrity.
  - Dara Knot: The Dara Knot is an ancient Celtic symbol, and can be traced back to antiquity to represent inner strength. It comes from the Gaelic Diore, which means oak tree, the Dara Knot is structured to reflect the roots of the mighty oak, as its roots need to maintain strength in order to hold up such a massive tree. This is very similar to how individuals must stay steadfast to preserve their integrity and inner strength.

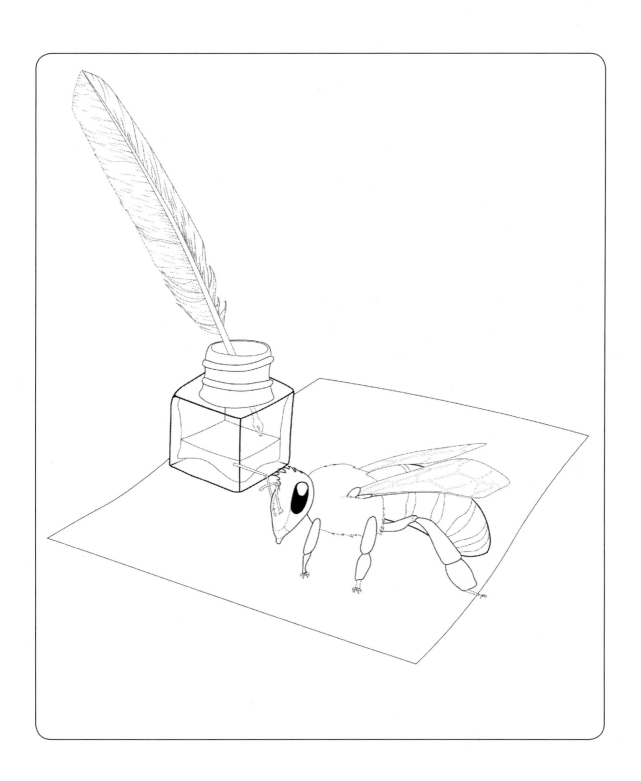

CHAPTER 6

BROW CHAKRA

- Wisdom
  - Owl – The owl has long been considered symbolic of wisdom. The origin of this symbolism is thought be in ancient Greek culture as Athena, the goddess of wisdom, was frequently depicted with an owl. Beyond this, it is believed that the owl's ability to see in the dark is another reason we associate it with wisdom.
  - Sapphire – The sapphire is known to be a stone of wisdom, along with being associated with royalty, divine favor, and prophecy. This gem is often provided to those who find themselves in need of spiritual clarity, insight and divine intervention.
  - Mala Beads – These beads are utilized by those who bear them as a tool for meditation seeing as they assist in focusing the mind, allowing them to achieve a higher awareness. It is for this reason that the mala beads have an association with wisdom along with clarity, divinity and higher consciousness.

- Knowledge
  - Tyet – The Tyet is an ancient Egyptian symbol that is associated with the goddess Isis, whose abilities of magical power were well known but not more so than her great knowledge. Her intellect was so vast that she was said to be cleverer than a million gods.
  - Spider – To the Akan people of Ghana, West Africa, the spider is a symbol of their god Anasi, considered as the god of all knowledge, who's physical form is said to be that of a spider.
  - Book – Books have long been associated with learning, knowledge, and insight since ancient times. Many educational institutions utilize the imagery of a book as their logo, and most religions consider their respective holy book to be a symbol and source of knowledge and enlightenment.

- Clairvoyance
  - Tarot Cards – Tarot cards have been used as early as the late 15th century and are used as a tool for mediumship by shuffling and cutting the deck before the user plays them out. The cards act as a mirror to an individual's soul, allowing the user to interpret them by looking peering within the intended target. They allow those with the knowledge to do so the ability to view aspects of an individual from a higher plane of existence that are hidden by the immediate physical realm.
  - Crystals – Crystals are stones that hold within them an energy that possesses the ability to effect the subconscious mind and even our emotions. Each crystal has its own meaning, as well as its own purpose for daily use. This provides one with the potential to invoke and manifest the life they desire.
  - Pendulum – Psychics utilize the pendulum as a sort of conduit to answer questions posed. The psychic relies on outside forces to manipulate the direction and severity of its swinging to provide answers to the desired question.

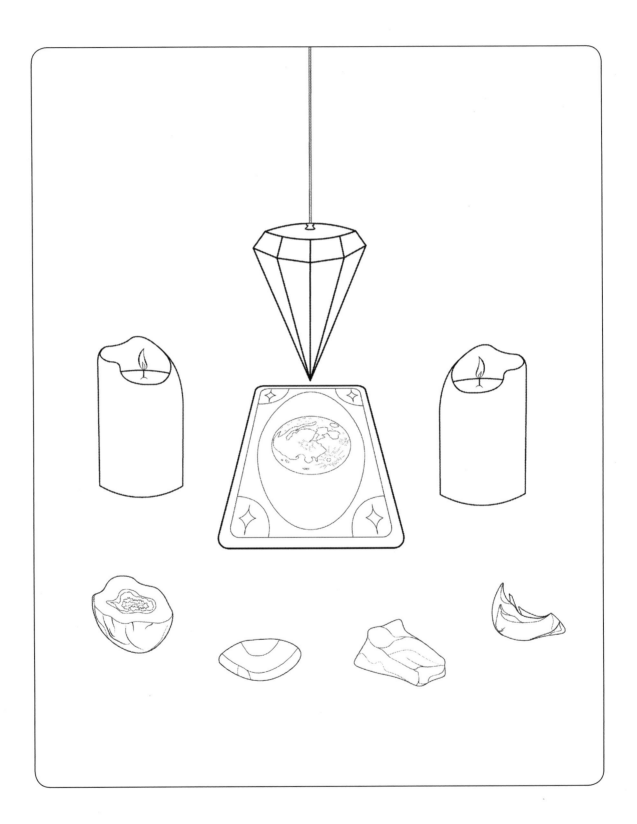

CHAPTER 7

CROWN CHAKRA

- Spirituality
  - Lotus: Known as the flower of awakening, the lotus begins its life cycle in the mud below the water. Slowly, it will ascend to the surface where its numerous petals blossom and open. It is this process that gives the flower its deeper meaning, serving as a powerful metaphor for our own spiritual journey. We all begin in a state of mental and spiritual darkness. Then, through hardship and perseverance, we reach a higher form of vitality through radiance and enlightenment.
  - The Hamsa Hand: This symbol is a one that originates from the ancient middle east that has been utilized through many different belief systems. Evidenced through archeological excavations, the hamsa predates the religions that use it today with experts believing that it comes from the Phoenicians where it served as a symbol of protection from an ancient goddess.
  - Eye of Horus: This ancient Egyptian symbol serves as a symbol of abundance and protection from the divine. The Eye of Horus is made up of six distinct parts, each meant to represent the human senses; hearing, sight, smell, taste, touch, and thought.

- Beauty
  - Cherry Blossom: Due to the entrancing spectacle they provide when they are in full bloom, the cherry blossom is a flower that has long been considered as a symbol of beauty; fleeting beauty in particular. The reasoning for this distinction coming from their life span and blooming beauty only lasting about 2 weeks.
  - Swan: The swan has been thought of as symbolic to beauty for thousands of years. In the tales of ancient Greek mythology, the swan was considered to be sacred to Aphrodite and Apollo, who were among the gods considered to be the personification of beauty.

- Bliss
  - Laughing Buddha: The laughing Buddha is often depicted with a large potbelly, and a large smile. The belly is meant to represent abundance and wealth while the smile, along with his leisurely position, serves to symbolize a glad and joyful state of peace and contentment.
  - Wunjo Rune: This runic symbol is one of ancient Nordic origin and is used to represent joy and acceptance. When utilized for prophetic purposes, its appearance is an indication of an era of brevity and following a depressive period of hardship or despair.
  - Yin-yang: The Yin-yang is a Chinese symbol that is meant to describe opposite, but interconnection forces of dark and light. These forces coexist in a state of duality, and their constant circling represent harmonious nature of the elements that make up our reality

Printed in the United States
by Baker & Taylor Publisher Services